THORNY DEVIL LIZARDS

AND OTHER *EXTREME* REPTILE ADAPTATIONS

by Lisa J. Amstutz

Consultant:
Joe Maierhauser, President & CEO
Terry Phillip, Curator of Reptiles
Reptile Gardens
Rapid City, South Dakota

CAPSTONE PRESS
a capstone imprint

T0052477

Fact Finders Books are published by Capstone Press,
1710 Roe Crest Drive, North Mankato, Minnesota 56003
www.capstonepub.com

Library of Congress Cataloging-in-Publication Data
Amstutz, Lisa J. author.
  Thorny devil lizards and other extreme reptile adaptations / by Lisa J. Amstutz.
     pages cm. — (Fact finders. Extreme adaptations)
  Summary: "Explores various extreme reptile adaptations throughout the world, including flying snakes, horned
lizards, and chuckwallas"—Provided by publisher.
  Audience: Ages 8-10.
  Audience: Grades 4 to 6.
  Includes bibliographical references and index.
  ISBN 978-1-4914-0168-2 (library binding)
  ISBN 978-1-4914-0173-6 (paperback)
  ISBN 978-1-4914-0177-4 (eBook pdf)
1. Animals—Adaptation—Juvenile literature. 2. Reptiles—Anatomy—Juvenile literature. 3. Reptiles—Physiology—
Juvenile literature. 4. Adaptation (Biology)—Juvenile literature. I. Title.
  QH546.A47 2015
  597.914—dc23   2014006947

Developed and Produced by Focus Strategic Communications, Inc.
   Adrianna Edwards: project manager
   Ron Edwards, Jessica Pegis: editors
   Rob Scanlan: designer and compositor
   Diane Hartmann: media researcher
   Francine Geraci: copy editor and proofreader
   Wendy Scavuzzo: fact checker

Photo Credits
Alamy: David Wall, 15, imageBROKER, 22, Top-Pics TBK, 4; Dreamstime: Mgkuijpers, 6 (bottom); Getty Images/
DigitalVision, cover, 1; iStock: zimdingo1, 23; Matthew Muir, 21; Nature Picture Library: Barrie Britton, 6 (top), Bence
Mate, 13; Omid Mozaffari, 10; Shutterstock: Antti Pulkkinen, 12, Cathy Keifer, 18, creativex, 16, Dennis Donohue,
27, feathercollector, 8, kkaplin, 28–29, Lawrence Wee, 9, Matt Jeppson, 14, 19, Paul101, 25, piotrwzk, 21 (inset),
reptiles4all, 11, Sergey Uryadnikov, 24; Thinkstock: Digital Vision, 20; Deborah Crowle Illustrations, 17; Wikipedia:
Antoshin Konstantin, 26

Design Elements
Shutterstock: Aleks Melnik, Gordan, NEV, Nikiteev_Konstantin, Osvath Zsolt, Thumbelina

Printed in the United States   5735

TABLE OF CONTENTS

GOING TO EXTREMES

Have you ever heard of a flying snake? Or a lizard that can walk on water? Amazing **adaptations** like these help reptiles survive even in extreme conditions. An adaptation is a body part or a behavior that helps an animal survive in its environment.

THE NEW ZEALAND TUATARA IS A RARE REPTILE.

Reptiles have backbones and lungs. Their skin is dry, scaly, and tough. Reptiles usually lay eggs on land, but a few give birth to live young. They are **cold-blooded**. This means their body is about the same temperature as the air around them. They must warm up or cool down by moving in and out of the sun. Reptiles live almost everywhere except the Arctic and Antarctic.

Reptiles include lizards and snakes, alligators and crocodiles, turtles and tortoises, and tuataras. In total, there are more than 8,000 living reptile **species**. Over time each group has adapted to its environment. Reptiles have developed amazing ways to find food and water, avoid **predators**, stay warm (or cool), and find a mate.

adaptation—a change a living thing goes through to better fit in with its environment

cold-blooded—having a body temperature that changes with the surroundings

species—a group of animals with similar features

predator—an animal that hunts other animals for food

FACT

The tuatara is a rare reptile found in New Zealand. Only two living species of tuatara remain. The word "tuatara" comes from the Maori language. It means "peaks on the back."

CHAPTER ONE

ON THE HUNT

Some adaptations help animals catch food. The egg-eating snake from Africa can eat eggs four times larger than its own head. Its thick gums grip the egg like suction cups. The snake moves its head back and forth to pierce the eggshell with special spines in its throat. It swallows the liquid inside. Then it spits out the shell.

A TINY *BROOKESIA MICRA* SITS ON A FINGER. IT IS THE SMALLEST REPTILE IN THE WORLD.

THIS EGG-EATING SNAKE JUST SWALLOWED AN EGG WHOLE!

The North American alligator snapping turtle can't swim very fast. So it tricks fish into swimming into its mouth. A small growth on the turtle's tongue looks like a worm. The turtle lies very still. It opens its mouth and wiggles its bait. A hungry fish comes looking for a meal. SNAP! It becomes the meal instead.

The world's smallest reptile is the *Brookesia micra*, a chameleon from Madagascar. It is so small it could perch on your fingertip! But the tiny lizard is a mighty hunter. Its eyes swivel in different directions, so it can look for **prey** without even turning its head. Its tongue shoots out to snag an insect faster than the blink of an eye.

prey—an animal hunted by another animal for food

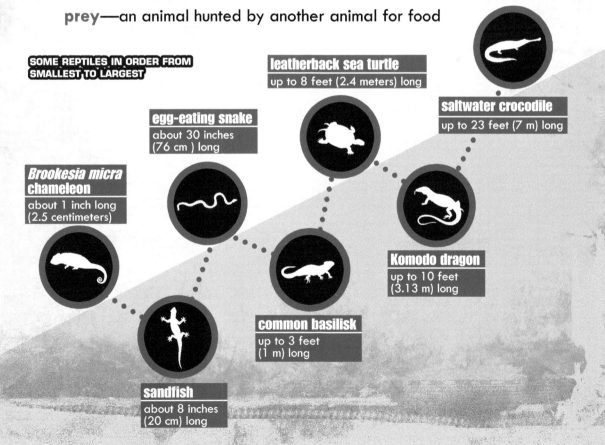

SOME REPTILES IN ORDER FROM SMALLEST TO LARGEST

leatherback sea turtle
up to 8 feet (2.4 meters) long

saltwater crocodile
up to 23 feet (7 m) long

egg-eating snake
about 30 inches (76 cm) long

Brookesia micra chameleon
about 1 inch long (2.5 centimeters)

Komodo dragon
up to 10 feet (3.13 m) long

common basilisk
up to 3 feet (1 m) long

sandfish
about 8 inches (20 cm) long

WINGED WONDERS

Is it a bird? Is it a plane? No, it's a reptile! Dangers lurk in the shadows of the rain forest floor. So these reptiles take to the air to stay safe.

The flying dragon of Southeast Asia lives in the rain forest **canopy**. It comes to the ground only to lay eggs. The flying dragon doesn't actually fly—it glides from tree to tree. As it leaps into the air, its ribs stretch out a flap of skin like an umbrella. It can glide 30–150 feet (9–46 m) without losing much height.

A FLYING DRAGON SHOWS OFF THE SKIN FLAP THAT LETS IT GLIDE.

FACT

Male flying dragons also show off their brightly colored "wings" to attract females.

To travel quickly through the jungle, the flying snake of Southeast Asia turns its body into the shape of a flying saucer. It flattens out its ribs, then glides through the air. Flying snakes have been known to sail 780 feet (238 m). That's longer than two football fields!

canopy—the middle layer of the rain forest where the greenery is thick and there is little sunlight

A FLYING SNAKE DANGLES FROM A TREE BRANCH BEFORE GLIDING THROUGH THE AIR.

EXTREME HUNTERS

A bird swoops down to gobble up a spider. Too late! It's a trick! The spider-tailed horned viper of Iran is adapted to lure its prey by wriggling the tip of its tail, which looks just like a spider. When prey comes near, the snake sinks in its **fangs**.

SPIDER-TAILED HORNED VIPER OF IRAN

FACT

A pit viper's fang acts just like a syringe. Venom moves through the middle of the fang into the prey's flesh.

Belcher's sea snakes are some of the most **venomous** of all snakes. Their deadly venom attacks the nervous system and lungs of its prey. Soon the victim can no longer breathe.

fang—a long, pointed tooth
venomous—able to produce a poison called venom

A PIT VIPER'S FANGS ARE STORED IN THE ROOF OF ITS MOUTH.

CHAPTER TWO

PLAYING DEFENSE

FANCY FOOTWORK

Upside down, right side up—it's all the same to a Tokay gecko. This superhero of the reptile world scurries along damp, slippery rain forest branches to find food and escape predators. Its sticky feet let it climb almost anywhere. What makes gecko feet so sticky? Billions of tiny hairs in their footpads!

Tiny forces make the hairs stick to the branches. The force is so strong the gecko can hang by one toe.

FACT

Scientists have made a material that sticks like gecko feet. In the future it may be used to make waterproof bandages. It might even hang a TV on a wall!

STICK AROUND! THE TOKAY GECKO SHOWS HOW TO STICK TO A TREE.

The basilisk of South and Central America runs on water to escape danger. This lizard lives in trees beside rivers. When a predator comes near, it drops to the water and speeds away. Fringed scales on its long toes spread out when the animal hits the water. A basilisk runs so fast it creates tiny air pockets in its feet that hold it up. A 175-pound (79-kilogram) human would need to run 65 miles (105 kilometers) per hour to do the same. If the lizard slows down, it will sink.

THE BASILISK TALES

The ancient Romans told stories about another kind of basilisk. This fire-breathing snake could kill with a look. Many people in the Middle Ages thought that only the crow of a rooster could kill a basilisk. Some travelers carried roosters to protect themselves.

THE BASILISK OF SOUTH AND CENTRAL AMERICA MAKES WALKING ON WATER LOOK EASY.

KEEP AWAY!

Horned lizards may not look tasty to you. However, many predators would disagree. Roadrunners, snakes, and coyotes are just a few of the animals that eat horned lizards.

The horned lizard defends itself in several ways. First it uses **camouflage**. Its brown speckled skin is hard to see in the desert sand. The lizard also puffs up so that its horn sticks out. If all else fails, the animal has one last trick— shooting blood from its eyeballs. The blood sprays up to 4 feet (1.2 m) away! The blood tastes bad to predators.

camouflage—a pattern or color on an animal's skin that makes it blend in with the things around it

habitat—the natural place and conditions in which a plant or animal lives

CAMOUFLAGE MAKES THESE HORNED LIZARDS BLEND IN WITH THE SAND AND ROCKS.

The thorny devil of Australia is one scary-looking critter. Even its scientific name sounds frightening: *Moloch horridus*. But this gentle lizard feeds only on ants. It eats up to 5,000 ants in one meal. The thorny devil's spikes protect it from predators. The spikes also collect dew that the lizard drinks. This is a useful adaptation in the animal's desert **habitat**, where every drop of water is precious.

THE THORNY DEVIL OF AUSTRALIA IS WELL ADAPTED TO LIVING IN THE DESERT.

EXTREME BEHAVIOR

Sometimes adaptations are not body parts, but special **behaviors**. The chuckwalla, a North American lizard, has an extreme way of avoiding predators. When danger comes near, the chuckwalla dives into a rocky crack and gulps air. Its body puffs up like a ball and becomes wedged in the crack. The animal's strong claws and rough skin keep it in place. Nothing can pull the chuckwalla out.

behavior—the way an animal acts

IS ANYBODY THERE? IF THE CHUCKWALLA SPOTS DANGER, IT DIVES INTO A CRACK AND PUFFS UP.

The world's largest turtle is a long-distance traveler. Leatherback turtles travel an average of 3,700 miles (6,000 km) from their breeding grounds to feeding grounds. The giant turtles lay their eggs on warm tropical beaches. Then the turtles travel north in search of jellyfish to eat.

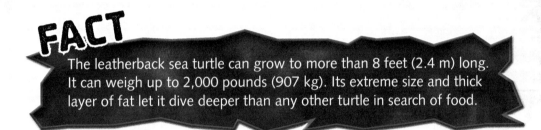

FACT

The leatherback sea turtle can grow to more than 8 feet (2.4 m) long. It can weigh up to 2,000 pounds (907 kg). Its extreme size and thick layer of fat let it dive deeper than any other turtle in search of food.

LEATHERBACK TURTLE TRAVEL

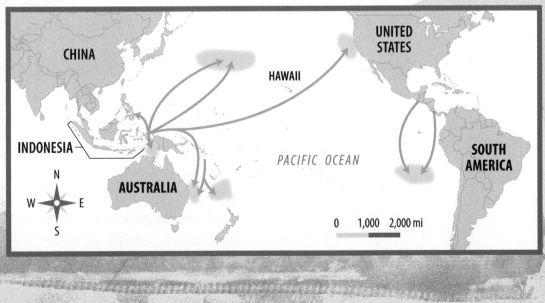

HIDE AND SEEK

Camouflage is an adaptation that helps some reptiles hide from predators and sneak up on prey. A leaf-tailed gecko looks exactly like a dried-up leaf or the bark of a tree. The gecko feeds at night, searching for insects and other small animals in the rain forests of Madagascar.

CAN YOU FIND THE TWO LEAF-TAILED GECKOS? THEY ARE DIFFICULT TO SPOT ON THE BARK OF A TREE.

Turtles don't move very fast, so catching speedy fish isn't easy. Leafy-looking flaps help the Matamata turtle of Brazil blend in with leaves and twigs in its river home. The submerged turtle pokes its pointed nose above the surface to breathe. When a fish gets close enough, the turtle snaps open its mouth, catching the unlucky fish.

The Madagascar leaf-nosed snake hides among leafy treetops. Its body is brown, just like a branch. The male's pointed snout looks like a twig. The female's head is leaf-shaped.

LIZARD TAILS

Many geckos and other lizards drop their tails when danger is near. Some even regrow new ones. The lizard tail has a zigzag line where it can pull apart. While a predator is chasing a lizard's tail, the lizard may be able to escape. If a viper strikes the tail, dropping it before the venom spreads may save the lizard's life.

THIS GECKO HAS DROPPED ITS TAIL.

SPITTING CRITTERS

Most reptiles run away or hide from predators. But the spitting cobra has another way of fending them off: It squirts venom at their eyes. The snake's aim is excellent.

The spitting cobra can shoot its venom up to 6.5 feet (2 m). The venom burns the predator's eyes, causing pain and even blindness. Meanwhile, the snake tries to escape. If that doesn't work, the snake can still bite.

TAKE AIM! THE SPITTING COBRA SHOOTS ITS VENOM.

One tricky lizard does not shoot venom, but it fools predators into thinking it will. Young Bushveld lizards **mimic** the oogpister beetle, which shoots acid at attackers' eyes. Bushveld lizards are the same color as the beetle and copy its walk. Predators may decide to stay away!

mimic—to copy the look, actions, or behaviors of another plant or animal

OOGPISTER BEETLE

BUSHVELD LIZARD

CHAPTER THREE

GIANTS OF THE REPTILE WORLD

One gentle giant, the Galapagos tortoise, lives on land. It can reach more than 5 feet (1.5 m) in length. It often weighs up to 550 pounds (250 kg). The tortoise's extreme size allows it to thrive in the hot, dry climate of the Galapagos Islands. It can store enough fat and water to survive without food or water for a year.

THE GALAPAGOS TORTOISE STORES FOOD AND WATER IN ITS BODY SO IT DOESN'T NEED TO EAT OR DRINK SO OFTEN.

But this adaptation has a downside for the tortoise. Each tortoise provides lots of meat and drinkable water to predators. Humans, and the animals they brought with them to the Galapagos Islands, nearly caused the tortoises to become **extinct**. Scientists are now working to save them.

A GALAPAGOS TORTOISE AND A BIRD

extinct—no longer living; an extinct animal is one that has died out with no more of its kind

FACT

The Galapagos tortoise and certain birds help each other out. The tortoise stretches out its legs and neck. It lets the birds clean off ticks and insects that it can't reach. In return, the birds get a free meal.

NOT-SO-GENTLE GIANTS

It may not breathe fire like a fairy-tale dragon, but the Komodo dragon is almost as fearsome. Komodo dragons live on four Indonesian islands. This giant lizard can grow to more than 10 feet (3.1 m) long. Because the lizard is so large, it can kill and eat almost anything.

Komodo dragons hunt pigs, goats, snakes, and dead animals. They are so big and strong they can even kill a 1,300-pound (590-kg) water buffalo. Komodos sometimes eat their own young as well. Young lizards may roll in the smelly guts of their prey or hide in bushes or trees to avoid being eaten. Komodo dragons have also been known to attack humans, but these cases are rare.

Animals bitten by a Komodo dragon usually die quickly. Komodo venom causes a rapid drop in blood pressure and massive bleeding, leading to death.

THE KOMODO DRAGON IS STRONG AND FIERCE.

The saltwater crocodile is the world's largest living reptile. It can grow to about 23 feet (7 m) long and weigh 2,200 pounds (1,000 kg). The crocs' powerful tails push their heavy bodies through the water. Their tails are so strong that crocs have been known to "walk" on their tails in the water. This adaptation may help them reach small animals in trees by the river's edge.

ENORMOUS ANCESTORS

Despite their giant size, Komodos and crocodiles are tiny compared to some of their ancestors. Scientists recently found fossils of a snake that makes today's giant boas look like earthworms. Titanoboa was as long as a school bus. It weighed as much as 20 people and lived in the swampy jungles of Colombia. It probably ate giant turtles and crocodiles.

WALKING ON ITS TAIL, A SALTWATER CROCODILE HUNTS FOR LUNCH.

CHAPTER FOUR

DESERT DWELLERS

The desert is hot and dry. Desert animals must find ways to keep their bodies cool. They must find food and water. And of course, they must find ways to stay safe.

The toad-headed agama lives in Asia. To scare away predators, it flashes its brightly colored mouth flaps. It can also vibrate its body to bury itself in the sand.

THE TOAD-HEADED AGAMA

The Mexican mole lizard is so well adapted to living underground that it has no back legs at all. It looks like a worm except for two little legs with long, sharp claws for digging. During the day the mole lizard hunts for insects underground. At night it comes to the surface to hunt.

The sandfish is not a fish but a sand-swimming lizard. Its smooth, shiny **scales** let it slip easily through the desert sands of Africa. This adaptation helps the lizard stay cool, escape predators, and catch insects. Fringes at the edges of its toes help it **burrow**. Small nostrils keep sand out of its nose.

scales—small, hard plates that cover the skin of reptiles

burrow—to dig a tunnel or hole in the ground

THE SANDFISH "SWIMS" IN THE SAND TO STAY COOL AND ESCAPE PREDATORS.

FACT

Scientists used X-rays to learn how the sandfish moves through sand. They found that it wriggles its body like a snake to "swim" through the sand.

CHAPTER FIVE

PAIRING OFF

FRILLED LIZARD

Some adaptations help an animal attract a mate. The male gharial of Asia, a crocodile relative, has a long, narrow snout with large bumps at the tip. The gharial uses it to make humming sounds and blow bubbles to attract a female.

Sometimes adaptations serve more than one purpose. The frilled lizard's huge, brightly colored neck flaps help scare off predators. The lizard spreads out its frill to look much larger and fiercer than it actually is. Males also use their frills to compete with other males for female attention.

Reptiles adapt to changes in their environments. Their amazing adaptations help them survive. Scientists learn more each day about how these adaptations work. Their research can result in new products or medicines. It can also teach people more about the world and how to protect it.

GLOSSARY

adaptation (a-dap-TAY-shuhn)—a change a living thing goes through to better fit in with its environment

behavior (bee-HAY-vyuhr)—the way an animal acts

burrow (BUHR-oh)—to dig a tunnel or hole in the ground

camouflage (KA-muh-flahzh)—a pattern or color on an animal's skin that makes it blend in with the things around it

canopy (KA-nuh-pee)—the middle layer of the rain forest where the greenery is thick and there is little sunlight

cold-blooded (KOHLD-BLUH-duhd)—having a body temperature that changes with the surroundings

extinct (ik-STINGKT)—no longer living; an extinct animal is one that has died out with no more of its kind

fang (FANG)—a long, pointed tooth

habitat (HAB-uh-tat)—the natural place and conditions in which a plant or animal lives

mimic (MIM-ik)—to copy the look, actions, or behaviors of another plant or animal

predator (PRED-uh-tur)—an animal that hunts other animals for food

prey (PRAY)—an animal hunted by another animal for food

scales (SKALES)—small, hard plates that cover the skin of reptiles

species (SPEE-sheez)—a group of animals with similar features

venomous (VEN-uhm-us)—able to produce a poison called venom

READ MORE

Bishop, Nic. *Snakes*. New York: Scholastic, 2012.

Holland, Simon. *Reptiles*. New York: DK, 2013.

Weber, Belinda. *Reptiles*. Discover Science. New York: Kingfisher, 2011.

Woodward, John. *Everything You Need to Know About Snakes and Other Scaly Reptiles*. New York: DK Publishing, 2013.

CRITICAL THINKING
USING THE COMMON CORE

1. Reread the section Keep Away! on page 14. What are three ways the horned lizard can defend itself? Give specific details from the text. Why do you think it has three ways, not just one? (Key Ideas and Details)

2. On page 5 the author wrote, "Reptiles live almost everywhere except the Arctic and Antarctic." Why can't reptiles live in the Arctic and Antarctic? Use details from the text to explain your answer. (Key Ideas and Details and Integration of Knowledge and Ideas)

3. Look at the diagram on page 7. What is this feature telling you? What is the most important information about reptiles in this diagram? Why did the author use a picture and not a paragraph? (Integration of Knowledge and Ideas)

INTERNET SITES

FactHound offers a safe, fun way to find Internet sites related to this book. All of the sites on FactHound have been researched by our staff.

Here's all you do:

Visit *www.facthound.com*

Type in this code: 9781491401682

 **Super-cool stuff!** Check out projects, games, and lots more at **www.capstonekids.com**

INDEX